T0064706

ORAL CANCER:

My Journey

The Simple Things Almost Lost

CHRISTINE DICKINSON

ARCHWAY
PUBLISHING

Cover photo and author photo courtesy of Cory Dickinson

Archway Publishing books may be ordered through booksellers or by contacting:

Archway Publishing
1663 Liberty Drive
Bloomington, IN 47403
www.archwaypublishing.com
1 (888) 242-5904

ISBN: 978-1-4808-4912-9 (sc)
ISBN: 978-1-4808-4913-6 (e)

Library of Congress Control Number: 2017910014

Print information available on the last page.

Archway Publishing rev. date: 07/11/2017

In Memory

This book is written in memory of Ryan Keck and Cathy Duttry, along with the many others who have lost their battle to oral (tongue) cancer.

Ryan was a very sweet young man who had tongue cancer. I had the privilege and honor of meeting him in March of 2015 at a local benefit that was held for him. During the short time I visited with him and his family, I learned of his strong faith and positive attitude. I kept in contact with him via texting for a few months. Ryan passed away on June 19, 2015, leaving his wife, a two-year-old son, and baby girl on the way. Ryan was only twenty-six years old.

Cathy was a beautiful mother of two toddlers. She always had a smile, along with a sense of humor. I had the honor of speaking at Cathy's benefit in July 2016. We kept in touch afterward via texting. Even though she was struggling through her treatments, Cathy maintained her sense of humor. God took his angel on December 7, 2016. Cathy was thirty-three years old.

It is so heartbreaking that these beautiful people never had the opportunity to eat food again after treatments and before leaving us. They both passed away a few months after completing their radiation and chemotherapy treatments. Because of Ryan, Cathy, and other oral, head, and neck cancer patients, we need to annihilate it—and all kinds of cancer—once and for all, so no one has to suffer. I wish I could wrap my arms around those suffering and make it all go away. We cannot lose more people to this monstrous beast.

Preface

I live in Emporium, Pennsylvania, a very small town with two traffic lights and a main street actually named Fourth Street. It is located approximately one hundred miles west-northwest of Williamsport, Pennsylvania. If you blink, you will have gone through town. Emporium is a borough and the county seat of Cameron County. As of 2010, the total population of Cameron County was 5,085, making it the least populated county in Pennsylvania.

I have lived here happily most of my life, until the day I found out I had tongue cancer. The majority of people in Emporium, or anyplace else for that matter, have never heard of oral cancer. Oral cancer has not received as much publicity and awareness as breast, prostate, and lung cancers, to name a few. Every year, approximately 25,000 people will be diagnosed with oral cancer in the United States. The most common being cancer of the tongue. These cancers generally occur in the following sites: tongue, tonsils and oropharynx (middle part of the throat), the gums, floor of the mouth, upper and lower jaw bony ridges, roof of the mouth, salivary glands, and so on. Most are caused by smoking (75 percent), tobacco use, and HPV (human papillomavirus infection). A small percentage (7 percent) is viral or unknown. Many survivors do not have a good quality of life. Oral, head, and neck cancers are profoundly different from other cancers. They affect one's ability to speak, swallow, and breathe. Many survivors live with feeding tubes (PEG, G-tubes), making eating difficult as well. Some patients live with permanent physical damage and disfigurement. Oral, head, and neck cancers are debilitating.

Our tongues have movable muscles, enabling us to eat and drink. Our cheeks and tongues work together to move food between the teeth to chew. The tongue presses food against the roof of the mouth. Chewed food is swallowed and moves along to the throat. Tongue movements touch glands that create saliva, which begins the predigestion process. The result is that we can taste the sweetness of a strawberry or chocolate, or the sourness of a lemon. Tongue cancer limits these everyday functions and often takes lives.

My purpose in writing this book is to make the public more aware of oral cancers based on personal experience. I am not sugarcoating anything in my book. I had stage IV—a squamous cell carcinoma involving the left side of my tongue. Squamous cell carcinoma is defined as an uncontrolled growth of abnormal cells; a malignant tumor that is locally invasive and has the potential to spread to other organs of the body as stated on the American Cancer Society's website, WebMD, and Cancer Centers of America. Stage IV indicates the cancer has grown more deeply into nearby tissue and may have spread to the lymph nodes.

At first, I was hesitant to write this book because I would be sharing intimate details of what I went through. I am not a writer, nor do I profess to be one, but I feel I must get my story out. A former colleague told me to move on and forget about the cancer episode of my life. However, I can't. I feel the need to share my story to provide hope and inspiration to others. I fought the toughest battle of my life. I may make you laugh and cry. And you may think I am bonkers, so be it. What people say about me behind my back or think of me means nothing. If I can help inspire one person with the story of what I felt, experienced, and witnessed, I have accomplished my goal.

This book is dedicated first and foremost to my mother, Theresia (Tilly) Germer Hutton, who passed away January 28, 2008, from breast cancer. I am so grateful that her old German stubbornness, strength, and sense of humor passed on to me. These traits helped me tremendously in going through my bump in the road. Second, I dedicate this book to Dr. Hassan Arshad, his staff, and the team of doctors and nurses on the seventh floor of Roswell Park Cancer Institute in Buffalo, New York. I want to give back to Roswell Park Cancer Institute for giving me back my life, so I am donating a portion of the proceeds of my book to Roswell for research and patient care for oral, head, and neck cancers. We need to eradicate this horrible, debilitating disease once and for all.

Chapter 1

IN SHOCK

*B*eep, beep, beep, whoosh, whoosh ... What are those sounds, and where are they coming from? Where am I? Am I dreaming? I wake up in a semi-dark hospital room, sitting in a reclining chair with IVs in my arms and feet. Oh my, I look like an octopus. I feel like I have been hit by a 747. This is not a dream but my reality. Why am I here, hooked up to all sorts of machines? Wait a minute ... it is coming back to me. I have cancer and am at Roswell Park Cancer Institute.

That painful, confusing awakening had its beginnings in the summer of 2011, when I first felt an annoying canker sore on the left side of my tongue. I repeatedly bit my tongue in the same spot. I rinsed my mouth with saltwater, peroxide, baking soda, and any canker sore medication I could pick up at my local drugstore. Nothing worked to alleviate the redness or soreness. It was becoming difficult to eat certain foods. At my regular dental checkup in early January 2012, I complained to my dentist that I was continuously biting my tongue, which was not healing. He gave me a prescription for a synthetic corticosteroid to put on the sore every evening for a week.

After a week, still no relief. So a biopsy was scheduled for January 17, 2012, at the Gundlah Dental Center in Olean, New York. The biopsy was not pleasant. The oral surgeon gave me a couple shots of novocaine to numb my tongue … ouch! A small chunk from the left side of my tongue was cut out and my tongue stitched up. I needed to get rid of this annoying problem prior to my vacation the first week in March.

My appointment arrived to finally obtain my results. The wait seemed like an eternity. It was a dark, dreary, wintery day. The dental office was bright and cheery compared to my dark mood. My sense of foreboding grew stronger as each minute ticked away in the waiting room. When I heard it was cancer, I gasped. My life was ending. Everyone I knew who had cancer died, including my mother. I told the oral surgeon I was scared and didn't want to die. After hearing the news, nothing seemed important.

I felt healthy and could not believe the news. *How can this be?* I never smoked or chewed tobacco, and I only had a couple drinks during holidays or on special occasions. I was told to see an oncologist and was given the choice of going to Pittsburgh or to the Roswell Park Cancer Institute in Buffalo for a consultation/treatment. I chose the latter because I had heard so many good things about Roswell.

I left the office and sat in my car in the parking lot, sobbing. Dark clouds loomed above as if they were telling me bad days lie ahead. Everything around me seemed to be a blur. My heart raced and I felt nauseated. My world was ending. I texted my friend Bea, who responded with, "If you want to scream go ahead." I couldn't scream. I was numb and in shock. I wiped away my tears and returned to work, pretending that everything was good. I felt ashamed that I had cancer and wanted to hide. I had always been a strong person and couldn't let anyone see I was scared. I wanted my life to be back to normal.

That evening I told my husband. He appeared upset and told me he had a feeling it might be cancer. We sat in the kitchen and discussed my upcoming appointment. I did not break down in front of him. I could not let him see how upset and frightened I was. I had to be strong.

When it was time for my initial appointment with Dr. Arshad in Buffalo, my best friend since first grade, Vicki, went with my husband, John, and I for support. It seemed like an eternity sitting in the waiting room. I filled out the necessary paperwork while waiting. When it came to the question of how much I weighed, I inserted, "Too darn much." Of course, I had to include a little humor to ease my anxiety.

I first met with Dr. Gupta, who was a resident. I found out later that he would be the one making most of the morning rounds after my surgery. Dr. Arshad then came in to the examination room to see me. I was so nervous and almost shaking. I didn't want to be there. I wanted to cry but didn't want everyone to see what a baby I was. Dr. Arshad told me I needed surgery and that I was not going on vacation that year, but maybe I could the following year.

I was told surgery would be soon, and I had to schedule a PET scan. The PET scan—positron emission tomography—is an imaging test that uses a special dye with radioactive tracers that are injected into a vein in your arm. An IV is inserted into a vein and then injected with liquid radioactive material. The patient has to wait an hour or more while the material flows through the body. After that, the patient is put through a scanner similar to when having a CT scan.

While I was there, I had a video laryngoscopy done to detect whether any cancer had spread to my throat or nasal passages. The inside of my right nostril was sprayed with a numbing agent. Then a flexible scope with an extremely small video camera attached at the end of it was inserted into my nose. I was asked to swallow the scope down into my throat. This is a very unpleasant test. The video camera allows the doctor to view the back of the throat, voice box, and vocal cords. The sensation made me tear up and gag. There went all my eye makeup! I have always had a bad gag reflex. It felt like a roto-rooter going through my nostril and down my throat. But thank God, no other cancer was detected!

I found out during my second appointment with Dr. Arshad that the PET scan was not good news. My cancer had spread to the lymph nodes on the left side of my neck. Now, the surgery would be longer and more difficult to remove the cancer, rebuild my tongue and remove those nodes. Surgery would be ten hours or longer.

I listened as carefully as I could while Dr. Arshad methodically ticked through the procedures. I would essentially be having four surgeries: partial removal of the left side of my tongue (glossectomy) with removal of tendon, skin, nerves, and veins (to supply blood to my tongue) from forearm to rebuild my tongue (free flap); removal of skin from my thigh to replace skin from forearm (skin graft); and a neck dissection to remove cancerous lymph nodes. I would also have a trach tube inserted for breathing purposes because my tongue would be so swollen that I wouldn't be able to breathe on my own. My doctor asked me if I was left handed; I used to wear my watch on my left arm. I am right handed and do a lot of writing for my job. While I was there, the staff at Roswell explained how to clean and take care of the trach tube that would be inserted. I wanted absolutely no part of that.

Dr. Arshad explained that the surgery was not guaranteed to work. If not, I would need another surgery to remove the tendon, skin, veins, and nerves from my right arm to rebuild my tongue. I asked if my surgery would be done by robotics. Dr. Arshad assured me he will have no problem doing the surgery manually. I was afraid my jaw would be split to gain easier access to the cancer on and in my tongue, but that won't be the case. Thank God! I was also checked out by the dental clinic. They were kind enough to schedule my pre-op tests while I was there, so I didn't have to make an extra trip. I told Dr. Arshad I had confidence in him, to which he replied, "So do I." At that point, I knew he was an awesome surgeon. Before leaving his office, I asked how long I would be in the hospital and was told probably a week to ten days. *You have got to be kidding*, I thought. I planned on being back to work in a week. I was never one to stay home during any illness, accident, or inclement weather.

Chapter 2
HOSPITAL STAY

I could not think clearly the week prior to surgery. I tried to get things organized at my office, thinking I would be back in a couple weeks. I was always a workaholic, competing with myself to see how many hours I could work in a week. I didn't sleep much. I believe my immune system was out of whack from not taking care of my health. I didn't eat healthfully, skipping meals on many occasions; and I was overweight. I was still depressed due to losing my nephew in 2005 and my mother in 2008. Wow, there were times when I worked an extra two or three months or more per year. One of my colleagues told my friend Bea (who also used to be a workaholic) and me that our tombstones should say, "If only I could have worked one more day." Yes, no one could top my hours. The day before my surgery, I packed my clothes and made out checks for bills to be paid while I was away. My husband, sister-in-law Donna, and her husband, Mike, were going with me. I gave my son a hug and cried, hanging onto him, not wanting to let go. As I left my house, I turned around, looked at everything in its familiar settings, and was sad. Would I be returning? Would I see my son again? I was going to undergo a full-day surgery and wondered if I would awaken afterward. I didn't want to leave my son or my home. I wanted to stay in the worst way, but I had to tackle this damn cancer that was trying to take over my life.

I hopped in the driver's seat and headed to Buffalo, trying to act as if we were all just going on an outing. I didn't want my passengers to see how distraught I truly was. The trip took a little over three and a half hours. We made it to Roswell Park Cancer Institute around 4:00 p.m. and headed to the Doubletree by Hilton Hotel, which is connected to Roswell and Buffalo General Hospital. My family checked in, and we entered our rooms; me with dread. I wished we were here for just a visit to explore Buffalo and not for my surgery. *Oh, how I am dreading this,* I thought.

While unpacking, we discussed where to have dinner. We didn't want to leave the hospital or hotel because we didn't know our way around Buffalo. The hotel clerk told us they had a restaurant named Carlton's Grill within the hotel. That night we had a nice dinner at Carlton's Grill. The staff was very friendly. I had the best open-faced turkey sandwich with gravy and mashed potatoes. Dinner was so good. I didn't talk much because I was thinking about my surgery in the morning. *Why do I have to go through this?* Little did I know that I would not be eating again for an extremely long time. I refer to this dinner now as my "last supper."

That evening, my family sat up watching a little television and talking. I couldn't relax. My head was spinning with thoughts like, *What if I don't wake up?* I watched TV but couldn't focus on what I was watching. I was going to be knocked out for a whole day, and you just never know what may happen. I still had more things I wanted to experience in my life. These repetitive thoughts occurred every few minutes. This had to be a dream! Soon, everyone was sleeping, and it was 2:00 a.m. *How can they sleep?* I couldn't sleep because maybe my life would be over. I thought about when Dr. Arshad asked if I was left handed. I grabbed some white paper from the tablet in my suitcase and wrote, "Do not touch my right arm." You hear periodically about mistakes being made during surgery, and I want to make damn sure it did not happen because of the writing I did in my job. I drifted off to sleep, waking up off and on, dreaming about my tongue being pulled out of my mouth and my teeth all being pulled. I didn't want to go through with the surgery. Could I back out of it now?

I woke up at 5:00 a.m., groggy, and showered. We all headed to the surgical unit, where I checked in. I felt as if I wanted to puke. I put on my gown, got up on the cot, and placed my sign across my chest. A nurse-anesthesiologist came in and started the IV drip and had me swallow some valium. I told her that it was not relaxing me at all. A little while later, I told her again. This time she added something to my IV and said she had a whole cabinet full of goodies for me. I told her I did not sleep well, to which she responded by telling me I would be having a long sleep.

My family came in after I am settled, and we talked a little. Finally, I felt a little drowsy but fought going to sleep. I wanted to be aware of what was going on around me. I must be in control of myself. No, I couldn't let myself sleep. I don't remember drifting off to sleep, but within a couple of minutes, the room was dark. It seemed more like I blacked out. My sister-in-law told me later that as I was being wheeled to the operating room, my "Do not touch my right arm" sign was still lying across my chest. From that day on, Dr. Arshad knew he had a nut on his hands.

I woke up in a reclining chair, barely able to focus, drifting in and out of sleep. I was extremely tired. My husband, sister-in-law, and her husband were looking at me. They were informed that I would be sleeping most of the day and came in to say goodbye because they were heading home. My sister-in-law and her husband live about four hours away from my house. My husband mentioned he would return to visit me during the weekend.

I found out that my surgery took fourteen hours, and I was kept sedated until the following morning, actually mid-morning, Wednesday, February 22. I was so exhausted; I just wanted to sleep.

One of the nurses came in and explained I was on a morphine pump and what button to push when I needed it. At this point, I couldn't care less about what was going on because all I wanted to do was sleep. I was still groggy, drifting in and out of sleep. I didn't even realize my family left my room. I did not get into bed but stayed in the recliner. Little did I know I would be spending seventeen days at Roswell Park Cancer Institute.

The next day a nurse came in and pulled a tube out from between my legs. She explained she was removing my catheter. I never realized I had one in. Now how in the hell did that get in there in the first place without me knowing about it? She placed a small whiteboard (dry-erase board) on my tray to write on. This was going to be my means of communication for a while because I wasn't able to talk. There was an IV in my arm and many other little tubes hanging out all over. It appeared I also had IVs in my feet, along with heavy stockings, which the nurse removed. She told me if I need anything to use my buzzer and then left my room.

I sat in my reclining chair. I felt as if I would choke if I lay on the bed. I slowly picked up the small mirror on my bedside tray. I was in shock and disbelief when I saw my reflection! I looked like some sort of horrible monster. Not that I was ever a thing of beauty, but this was gruesome! My face was swollen, as was my tongue, which hung out the right side of my mouth. Is it my tongue? Dear Lord, it is!

The left side of my neck is bandaged with what appeared to be tentacles hanging from it. My left forearm was accessorized with a cast. A trach tube was in my neck. My left thigh had a huge see-through plastic bandage on it, which was filled with blood. There's also a feeding tube stitched to my left nostril. I could easily get a part in a horror movie! Damn, I scared myself! I tried to watch television but couldn't concentrate. I was in pain, so I hit my morphine pump to fall back sleep and forget the nightmare I was living. Maybe this was just a dream, and I will wake up in my own bed.

On the second day following surgery, a nurse's aide came into my room and helped me to the bathroom. She handed me a package of disposable washcloths and told me I could wash myself near the sink. As she left the room, I glanced in the mirror and almost screamed in sheer terror because of the horror looking back at me. *This isn't me; it can't be. Oh my, I am a living nightmare!* I was weak but tried to wash myself with my right hand. I couldn't do it. I felt as if I was going to pass out. I was alone, with no family or friends. I missed everyone and started crying.

A young nurse entered the bathroom, asking if I need help. (I learned later her name was Elizabeth McNamara.) I couldn't talk, so I nodded. She looked like an angel. I wrote on my whiteboard if I could have some tape and paper towels to cover up the bathroom mirror. My nurse obliged and taped the towels to the mirror. I certainly didn't want to frighten myself when going to the bathroom at night. I could possibly give myself a heart attack if I looked in the mirror. She helped wash me up and then assisted me back to my reclining chair.

I tried to watch TV, but it was so difficult to focus. Different nurses came in during the day and evening to take blood and administer a heparin shot twice a day to prevent clotting. I looked like a black-and-blue pin cushion after all that. I hoped I could go home in a few days and return to work.

Throughout my stay, a team of doctors came in first thing in the morning and checked on me. I recall seeing Dr. Arshad from time to time. Dr. Gupta usually made the morning rounds. I can't imagine the smell as he looked into my mouth, checking the surgical sites. My breath was atrocious and probably smelled like a dead animal alongside the road.

During my daily exams, a Doppler test was done on my tongue, checking to see if there was a pulse to make certain the tissue removed from my forearm was living. If there was no pulse, then another surgery would be required to remove the dead tissue, which would have to be removed from my right forearm. I always panicked during the exams. Thank God, the doctors always found a pulse! I could easily see and feel one big stitch in the front of my tongue because it was so grotesquely swollen. There were also many stitches along the middle and back of my tongue. I was given mouthwash to rinse my mouth several times a day, because I was not able to brush my teeth due to the surgery.

One morning my team of doctors came in and took off the cast bandaging on my left forearm. All I could see were tons of stitches and a bloody, hollowed out arm. One of the doctors mentioned how beautiful it looked. He had to be kidding! I grabbed my whiteboard and wrote that my arm looked more like one on Frankenstein's monster. It was very grotesque. I wondered, *Will I ever have full use of my arm again?*

After a few days, the tentacles (drain tubes) were removed from my neck. Then, within the next couple of days, I got an earache that became progressively worse as evening rolled around. I could not sleep. I tried lying on my bed to get comfortable, but it hurt worse, and I felt as if I would choke with my humongous tongue. I got off the bed and returned to my chair. By then, I was rocking myself back and forth from the pain. I buzzed for the nurse and wrote on my whiteboard that my left ear hurt, and I couldn't sleep. This was toward the first weekend of my stay. I found out that fluid backed up, causing an infection. So the tentacles were put back in the left side of my neck.

Finally, my trach was removed. It was so disgustingly gross to clean the buildup of mucus around the trach with the suction, so I seldom did it. Thank goodness I didn't have to deal with that any longer. I could finally breathe on my own. Hoorah!

My husband came up that Saturday and told me my face was very swollen on my left side. At that point, after scaring myself when I looked in the mirror the first time and with him telling me how swollen my face was due to the infection, I certainly didn't feel like having visitors. But my youngest brother, Tom, and his wife, Karen, came to see me that weekend also. My middle sister, Trudie, came with them. Karen was drinking an orange Sunkist soda. Oh, how my mouth was watering, knowing I could not have a drink. I love you, Karen, but I could have smacked you that day.

While they were visiting, I received a text from my friend Bea. Bea was an ex-client I worked for. We became friends and vowed to get together once a year. The text contained a video of herself, Jeri, and Cherie, waiting to board the plane, asking where I was because they were waiting for me. Jeri worked with Bea, and I got to know her through working with her as well. Cherie is an old school friend of Jeri's and has traveled with us before. In the video, they all yelled, "We miss you!" They were getting ready to fly to San Juan for the Royal Caribbean cruise I had to cancel. The tears started welling up in my eyes when I first saw their faces, and I sobbed openly in front of my siblings. This was so unfair!

The next morning I was so depressed and kept crying. I couldn't eat or talk. Why had this happened? What more did I have to endure? Had I done something so bad that God was punishing me? A volunteer came into my room with a selection of magazines to choose from. She noticed that I was upset and asked if there was anything she could do for me. I showed her what I had written on my whiteboard earlier that morning: "Am I a bad person? I never stole anything. I am not a criminal or murderer, child molester, and would never hurt anyone, so why do I have cancer? God must feel I am a horrible person and wants me to suffer. Why isn't this happening to those people? Why me?" The volunteer asked if she could get someone to talk to me. I wrote back, "No, I am just feeling sorry for myself. I will be okay after a while." I didn't want her to think I was nuts and needed counseling.

After a few days, my tentacles were removed from my neck. Maybe I was getting back to normal. I wanted some normalcy in my life in the worst way.

My nasal feeding tube became plugged at one point, the attending physician took out the stitches on my nose and pulled the tube out. Hopefully, I got rid of some nasty nostril hair. A new tube was inserted, which I had to help with by trying to swallow, gagging the entire time, and tears streaming down my face. The doctor was going to stitch it back onto my nostril. I was not having any part of that again! I quickly wrote on my whiteboard, "No more stitches!" So he taped it to my nostril and told me I had to be very careful not to pull it out, or I would have to have it stitched back on. Believe me, I wanted to pull everything out!

All this time, I wasn't eating but was being fed Ensure through the nasal feeding tube. Oh, how I so wanted a big, tall glass of milk at night. I could smell the food coming to the other patients for breakfast, lunch, and dinner, and it was difficult knowing I couldn't have anything. I was constantly thinking about when I would be able to order actual food.

Based on what I could hear in the hall, most patients had a selection of food to choose from. In order for the nasal feeding tube to be removed, I had to be able to swallow. I could not wait to hear the food cart coming just so I could smell the aroma of what I couldn't have. I wondered what was wrong with my progress. These patients were eating. Why couldn't I? But most of them had other kinds of surgeries.

One morning, approximately a week later, I was having the Doppler test on my tongue. My tongue still had a pulse! The doctor doing the exam told me, "Congratulations, you have a brand-new baby boy." What did that remark have to do with my tongue? What he was trying to tell me in a comical way was that the surgery was a success, and I had a living rebuilt tongue. He sure had a weird sense of humor. I can't remember who the doctor was, but he made me happy to know the graft worked. The next step was the swallow test, which I failed. I can't begin to tell you how frightening this was. I felt as if I would choke. I failed my test several times, so I couldn't go home yet. I had to be careful not to aspirate (swallowing food into lungs). I was looking forward to going home. Not good; can't go home. I began to cry because I was alone with no family or friends, and I missed them and my home. At that moment, I felt I would spend whatever was left of my life there in the hospital.

During one of my morning exams, one of the doctors told me that I could try to talk. Toward evening, I called my husband. He couldn't figure out who was trying to talk to him, nor could he make out the words. I bet he was thinking it was a prank caller. After a few minutes, he realized the voice on the other end was me. The poor guy was so surprised. I heard him crying, which started me crying. He told me that he thought I would never be able to speak again. My voice was extremely garbled, as if I had a mouthful of marbles. It was very difficult to pronounce words because my tongue was stiff, and I didn't have full use of it. *Would I always sound like this?*

My youngest sister, Sue, and her husband, Brian, came to visit me the following weekend. My sister is a hoot and can make everyone around her laugh. She asked one of the nurses if she could wash my hair. The nurse brought in one of those no-rinse shampoo caps. Sue gave me a nice scalp massage. I hadn't been able to shower or wash my hair; I could only wash up with disposable cleaning cloths. I enjoyed the shampoo tremendously but did not like the results. All the hair coloring I had done prior to surgery was gone, and the damn gray hair was shining through like a super LED light! Oh, dear, now I had the gray streaks to go along with my monstrous-looking face. At this rate, I could easily become one of the extras on *The Walking Dead*.

After about two weeks and during my husband's weekend visit, I still had difficulty swallowing. He mentioned to one of the nurses to let me try drinking the Ensure from the bottle. At the time, it was being fed to me via my nasal feeding tube. I tried but failed. The next day, my nurse Roberta came into my room with a pink, princess sippy cup like toddlers use. It was a beauty in my eyes. Roberta also brought in plastic baby spoons.

She told us that she thought and thought about how she could make it easier for me to swallow, thus the sippy cup. Roberta had bought the cup and spoons out of her own pocket. She was such an awesome nurse, going out of her own way to help me. She put a little water into the cup and handed it to me. At first, it was difficult because I felt like I was choking. But then swallowing became easier. After that, I had some ginger ale. Oh, my virgin tongue (the portion that was rebuilt with my forearm) wasn't a virgin any longer. It was awesome! Swallowing became easier, and I could drink my Ensure from the bottle. I finally got to order some food—broth—and worked my way up to Jell-O and pudding. However, my mainstay was Ensure for vitamins and protein. I also drank another protein drink, Isopure, daily.

My friend Vicki came to visit me one evening. She has quite a sense of humor and helped to lift my spirits. Vicki brought me a nice, cozy, pink robe. It was very comforting and made me feel safe. It also helped to cover my butt. During our visit, a nurse came into my room to let me know the head of the radiology department wanted to meet with me in the patient lounge. Vicki went with me for support. The patient lounge was very relaxing and cheery. There was a large window overlooking part of Buffalo, and I could see windmills on the shore of Lake Erie, bordering Buffalo.

Finally, the head of the radiology department, Dr. Singh, entered the lounge with his assistant. He informed me I would have to undergo approximately six weeks (thirty-three treatments) of radiation therapy. I asked about returning to work. His response was my new job was taking care of myself, and by doing so, I would have a better outcome. Dr. Singh suggested that I not return to work for a year. I was devastated. I planned on trying to work throughout my radiation treatments, but he said that was not a good idea. Vicki asked about chemo. She actually asked most of the questions because I was nervous. Since the cancer had spread to my lymph nodes on the left side of my neck, Dr. Singh said I would need chemo as well. My heart raced, and I felt as if I would vomit. *I do not want to lose my hair*, I thought. We women do not want to lose our crowning glory. Chemo generally causes total hair loss, but with certain chemo treatments there is just thinning. Dr. Singh explained that in about three weeks, or halfway into radiation therapy, things would get rough, and I would lose weight. I looked at him like he was nuts. I am a tough person with a high threshold of pain.

This doctor didn't know how damn tough I was! Then to top off the conversation, he told me I would have to have a feeding tube inserted while undergoing treatments. Hmmm? *You have got to be kidding! Why in the hell do I need a feeding tube?* I could swallow. Dr. Singh told me I could have the procedure done while in the hospital. I responded with no, I would wait. I didn't want a feeding tube hanging out of my stomach! His assistant said life by the inch is a cinch, and life by the yard is hard. They both explained that I will have a sore throat, mouth sores, and lose my taste for food. Radiation can also do a number on your teeth. Dr. Singh reiterated that it was my job to take care of myself and to use the mouthwash I was given every day. And absolutely no smoking. I don't know why that was even brought up. I never smoked. I was told if I did these things, I would have a better outcome. Vicki and I headed back to my room. I was so happy she was with me during the radiation consultation. Vicki reminded me on her way out the door to do what the doctor suggested. All I could think about that night while trying to sleep was about the darn feeding tube that would be inserted into my stomach. I didn't want one, and I didn't know what the big deal was. I had seen people who were undergoing radiation therapy, and they could eat with no problem. But I found out later they were not undergoing treatment for oral or head/neck cancer but for other cancers.

Throughout most of my hospital stay, I was hooked up to an IV, which was plugged into an outlet in the wall. During this time, I saw the physical therapist almost daily. He went with me the first couple of times for a walk around the west wing. Thereafter, I took off on my own. I would unplug the IV cord from the outlet and hold onto the IV pole for my walk. I soon became tired of my shadow. I wanted to rip that IV out. When I had the nasal feeding tube still in, I felt like one of those bulls with a ring through its nose. Not fun at all! It got easier to walk around with my shadow after my nasal feeding tube was removed.

I recall two times when I got up at night to use the bathroom, I accidentally scraped the plastic covering the skin graft on my left thigh with my fingernails. When I stood up, blood was seeping out onto the floor. I buzzed for the nurse. What a mess I made on the floor as well as on my hospital gown. Oh my, these gowns were so not the epitome of the fashion industry. I was frightened because I thought I would have to have another graft done. But no, all the nurse had to do was tape more plastic onto my thigh. This getting up to use the bathroom a few times per night was a pain.

Chapter 3

HOME

On March 9, 2012, I was finally discharged. Woohoo! Now maybe I could get back to normal. My husband and son came to pick me up. I hadn't seen my son since February 20. He wasn't able to visit during the weekends due to having the flu. I sat uncomfortably in the backseat of the jeep for my two and a half-hour journey home. We stopped at Tim Horton's to get an iced hazelnut coffee for me to try. It was so tasty.

After we arrived home, I got situated in my chair and waited for my six-year-old grandson, Kasey, to visit me. My son brought him into the house. The poor baby took one look at me, started crying, and headed upstairs to his bedroom to hide from me. I didn't blame him because I did not look like Grandma any longer. I looked like a monster, with my swollen tongue hanging out of my mouth and bandages on my neck and arm. I was heartbroken!

Grandma would never do anything to harm him, but I scared the hell out of him. What a horrific creature I looked like. I started sobbing uncontrollably. This little guy was my world! My husband talked to him and explained what happened to his grandma. Kasey finally made it downstairs to see me and gave me a hug. I cried again. He kept his distance from me for a while thereafter. That Easter, he looked at me one morning and said, "Grandma, I was afraid of you for a very long time, but now I'm not afraid. And when you get better, we can go outside and play." We went out that following winter, in 2013, and made snow angels. My Kasey was back, loving his grandma! Grandma had her baby back.

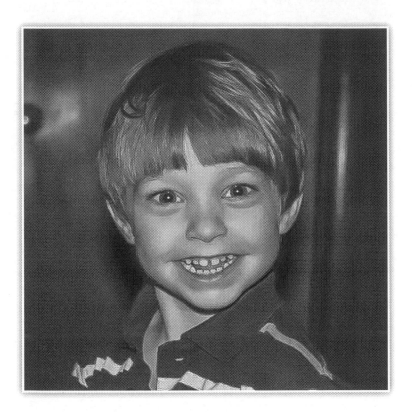

Kasey was born prematurely on September 15, 2005. His due date wasn't until the middle of November. He is such a little fighter and means the world to Grandma.

Chapter 4

RECUPERATION

*D*uring my time recuperating at home, visiting nurses came to see me daily, taking vitals and changing the dressings on my neck wound, wound from trach, forearm wound, and skin graft on thigh. I kept them busy for a while. I have never been a morning person and did not like getting up early for their visits. I just wanted to sleep and wished to be left alone, but I knew they had to take care of me. At that time, I was having cream of wheat for breakfast, clear broth for lunch, and instant mashed potatoes with lots of butter and gravy for dinner, along with my daily servings of several bottles of Ensure.

It was spring, and the robins were singing and building nests. My mother and I used to have a competition every year as to who would see the first robin. We had a few who would build a nest in the twig wreath on our front door or on our back deck. It was fun to watch them. That spring was strange because when I came downstairs for breakfast and walked into my kitchen and pass the sliding glass door to the deck, a robin constantly flew into the sliding glass door with such urgency. It was as if it wanted to attack me. It appeared to happen only when I walked past the door, and it did not react like that to anyone else in my family. Was it because my bandages made the bird think I was a monster, and it was trying to protect its nest? Or was my mother's spirit in the robin, wanting to come in and comfort me? I have heard of spirits in cardinals but not robins. It was very bizarre. This went on for a few weeks and then my robin finally left.

After a couple weeks, I headed back to Roswell to see Dr. Arshad for my follow-up appointment. My husband and Vicki accompanied me. It was then that I find out my surgery took fourteen hours. He explained that he did a partial left-sided glossectomy (surgical removal of tongue), extended lymph node dissection (removal of lymph nodes), and tracheostomy (an incision in the windpipe to insert a breathing tube). Staging was pT2N2b, meaning the primary tumor was larger than two centimeters but less than four centimeters, and cancer cells were present in the lymph nodes on same side of neck as primary tumor. It was stage IV-A; cancer had spread to the surrounding lymph nodes. The HPV 16/18 test—for human papillomavirus, which is one of the causes of oral, head, and neck cancers—was negative. I also had reconstruction of my left tongue and floor of mouth with a left radial forearm, free flap, split-thickness skin graft from left thigh. In other words, a flap of skin/muscle with blood veins and nerves was removed from my forearm to rebuild a portion of my tongue. Dr. Arshad told me I needed to start radiation and chemo and agreed I could do this in Olean, New York, instead of traveling to Buffalo daily. This would leave me with a little more than an hour drive from my house one way instead of two and a half hours to Buffalo. Dr. Arshad would contact Dr. Gregory Hare and Dr. Neeta Soni to schedule my treatments; both of their offices were associated with Roswell. I asked Dr. Arshad what he thought caused my cancer. His reply was no cause could be found. Then Vicki said, "Chris, it must have been that last chew you had that did it." She could always make me laugh.

I met with Dr. Hare on March 20, and we scheduled a simulation treatment at which time I would be measured for a face mask to be worn during treatment. He explained the treatment and the risks of radiation therapy, which were extensive. Head and neck postoperative radiation therapy can be quite morbid. This includes, in part, long-term

G-tube (gastronomy feeding tube) dependency due to permanent dysphagia (difficulty or discomfort in swallowing), osteoradionecrosis (traumatic fracture of maxillary jawbone), second malignancy risk, chronic pain, treatment failure, and chronic dry mouth. This was frightening to hear, but I decided to undergo treatment, which would entail thirty-three daily treatments, except weekends. Dr. Hare also recommended G-tube placement because, as he explained, things would get rough with swallowing/eating. I didn't want one when first approached in the hospital about its need during treatment, but we scheduled my G-tube placement at Olean General Hospital for the following week, on Tuesday, March 27. I would start radiation therapy on Monday, April 2, 2012. I was scared and didn't want to do this.

I also met with Dr. Neeta Soni and found out that I need to have a mediport. A mediport is a small medical appliance, or port, that is placed beneath the skin of the upper chest. The port has a septum (a partition separating two chambers) through which drugs can be injected or blood drawn. A catheter connects the port to a vein. The mediport would be inserted for chemo treatments. I needed all-day treatments using cisplatin, which could damage my kidneys. Treatment would be two hours of fluid, two hours of cisplatin, two hours of fluids, then cisplatin. My mediport insertion appointment would be done in the hospital on Thursday, March 29, two days after G-tube surgery. I would have my first chemo treatment on April 2, beginning at 8:00 a.m. I would then head to my radiation therapy, which would be close to 4:00 p.m. I only needed three chemo treatments— the first day of radiation, halfway through radiation, and the last day of radiation therapy. I was going to be a busy woman. I considered working between treatments and drive myself back and forth. I could do this!

March 27, 2012; time for my G-tube, or PEG tube, surgery. A numbing spray was sprayed into my mouth, and I was asked to try to swallow a tube down my throat to get the ball rolling. I have a very bad gag reflex and started choking. I asked for someone to please put me out during this. Finally, I drifted off into oblivion. When it was over, my stomach was sore, to say the least. A nurse explained to my husband how to clean around the tube and how to feed me. It's a wonder the poor guy didn't run away. I certainly wanted no part of this. I was told my stomach area would be sore for a week and to hold a pillow tightly across it when sitting down or standing up. On our way out of the hospital, a pleasant older gentleman (a greeter) handed me a carnation. It's my understanding that on discharge, they hand out carnations.

Back home, I tried to adjust to the feeding tube. I still believed I didn't need the damn thing. I had a heck of a time trying to sit and stand while holding a pillow tightly against my stomach as instructed. The pillow helped somewhat with the pain. I was depressed because I thought after surgery, I was all done and could get back to my life. No! First, I had tentacles hanging out of my neck at Roswell Park Cancer Institute, and now I had an appendage hanging out of my stomach. I had to keep the tube taped to my stomach when not in use. But when the tape came off, the darn tube would hang and show under my shirt. Plus, I had to remember to keep the clamp closed, or whatever I put through it came back out. My husband cleaned around my feeding tube for a week. John had so much patience. And all I wanted to do was rip it out.

On March 29, I returned to Olean General Hospital to get my mediport inserted. I had just about had it by then. Enough was enough! I did not want this. Why couldn't I have chemo by sticking a needle in a vein in my arm, like they do for labs? I was put into a semi-sleep state but drifted in and out of sleep. I could hear Dr. Mancl talking at times. She had to make an incision in my chest, just below my right collarbone, to insert the mediport. Now I had a sore chest to boot. Dr. Mancl did both my mediport and feeding tube surgeries. She is a fine, young, compassionate surgeon. I remember she rubbed my shoulder, telling me I did fine. On my way out of the hospital in a wheelchair (though I could walk fine), the same gentleman saw me and looked surprised. He asked if I would like another carnation. I told him I came back purposely for more surgery so that I could get another carnation. The nice gentleman didn't know what to think of me.

After both surgeries, I had difficulty getting in a comfortable position to sleep. I am a side sleeper, but when I tried to lie on my side, the mediport and feeding tube pinched. I had to lie on my back and try sleeping with propped up pillows. I never had any restful sleep after that. I wished this was all over with so I could get my life back to normal. I wanted to sleep normally. Would I ever be able to do so?

During this time, I still had visiting nurses come in to clean my neck wound, feeding tube, and mediport areas. I also had between three and four speech therapy sessions. It was getting increasingly difficult for me to get up in the morning due to lack of sleep. I can't sleep very well on my back. Even propping my head up on several pillows didn't help. I couldn't wait for the nurses to leave so I could try to go back to sleep. I was not using my feeding tube because I could drink my Ensure and eat my broth, mashed potatoes, and sometimes pudding.

I tried sitting on my front porch to enjoy the warm spring weather but was attacked by insects, gnats, flies, and so on. I was a total bug magnet. Leave it to me to attract the damn bugs. They landed on my left, scabbed forearm, neck, and upper thigh that were healing from surgery. Damn, I couldn't even enjoy sitting outside.

Chapter 5

TREATMENTS

$\mathcal{I}$ tolerated my first chemo and radiation treatments fine. The mediport area was a little sore, but I had no problems. So I assumed I would be able to go back to work and drive myself to and from. I was given medication a couple days before chemo to alleviate any nausea. One chemo treatment down with two more left, and thirty-two radiation treatments left. I thought, *This isn't so bad.* And I was still eating my mashed potatoes, pudding, and broth, and drinking Ensure. My tongue was still swollen but not like it was after surgery. I still cannot see my bottom teeth or brush my teeth yet. I use a prescription mouthwash several times per day.

Three and a half weeks later, all hell broke loose. I was so tired, all I wanted to do was sleep. I didn't want to get up in the mornings. My husband would wake me and tell me it was time to get ready for my radiation therapy. I didn't want to go. It was not fair. Please, please, let me sleep. My tongue felt more swollen, and I had issues with mucus. I had difficulty sleeping because of coughing and spitting up due to an overproduction of mucus. I got in the habit of falling asleep while going to and coming from my treatments due to staying up until 5:00 a.m. and later, watching *Golden Girls, I Love Lucy,* and *Frasier* repeats. I needed the laughs. When I woke up, I noticed hair on my pillow. This continued, with more hair stuck on my pillow daily. I was shocked to see this and would puke. I was lucky that I had thick hair. Eventually, I lost all the hair on the back of my head, but it only thinned on the top. I have one bald spot near the nape of my neck that has never grown back. I believe this is where my horns appear when I am bad.

It became difficult to lie still during my radiation therapy. The mucus wouldn't stop, and I felt as if I was choking. I had to lie perfectly still. I couldn't do this anymore; nor did I want to eat. I contracted thrush twice; I always thought only babies contracted thrush. My mouth and throat were sore. I am constantly spitting up into a tissue. It was time to resort to eating with my PEG tube, though it was the last thing I wanted to do. I was so sleep deprived at that point, which got progressively worse. I was prescribed a painkiller to help with the mouth sores and sore throat, but I no longer wanted to swallow. The painkillers caused constipation, and I was miserable from not being able to defecate for three days. Finally, I contacted my visiting nurse. She came with an enema and immediately eased my problem. I was so humiliated that I vowed no more painkillers ever again. I had enough of the crap I was going through and would never tolerate this ever again. I didn't like pain meds because they sort of put me in la-la land. I wanted to be 100 percent aware of what was going on around me, not in a state of stupor.

My second chemo treatment went fine. I noticed that when radiation therapy and chemo were on the same day, combined with my lack of sleep, I was drained physically. I was more sensitive to cold and always felt chilled, even when it was warm outside. I would have loved to stop my radiation treatments because the mucus was getting worse daily, my tongue was more swollen, and I had mouth sores and a sore throat. Could it get any worse than this? I still couldn't see my bottom teeth. About four and a half weeks into radiation, it got to the point that I cried as I went into the treatment room. The people at Mildred Milliman Radiation Medicine Center were so compassionate and caring, telling me it would get better. They would pat my back as I walked down the hall to the therapy room, telling me I could do this. The waiting room had a pleasant atmosphere, and everyone was so friendly and accommodating.

I broke down and asked if I could have some music to get my mind off the treatment. Mind you, the treatments didn't take long; nor were they painful. It was just so damn difficult to lie still with constant postnasal drip and mucus building up, making me feel I would choke. It was difficult to move my head because of the mask I had to wear, which was snapped onto the cot. I have always had some sort of seasonal and food allergies. My nose ran around cleaning products, being outside, and after drinking milk or eating dairy products, and so on. I believe this is why I had major mucus issues.

As soon as I returned to my house after radiation therapy, I crossed off the day on my calendar. Would I be able to make it through the next few weeks? I was told I could take a break and then continue again. I seriously thought about it but didn't want to prolong treatment. I wanted it over with as quickly as possible. My mouth was so sore, along with my throat. The skin on my neck was red, peeling, and oozing from radiation burns. Thank goodness for burn cream. Both sides of my neck were treated because I was informed the cancer could spread from the lymph nodes on the left side of my neck to those on the right side. I was so grateful to have no feeling on the left side due to the surgery. The nerves were dead, and I might not ever have feeling again on the left side of my neck. Dr. Hare had me try gargling with a concoction of baking soda, and so on to help alleviate mucus. He mentioned pain medication, but I refused. I was not going through the enema crap again. The concoction made me gag and puke. *I can't take much of this any longer,* I thought. *I am so damn tired of it all.* At this time, I was only getting nourishment through my feeding tube. Every morning I gargled with the concoction and ended up dry heaving and then puking. It got to the point that I dreaded even looking at the glass I mixed the concoction in. I contracted thrush again. I coughed up so much mucus/phlegm that I puked constantly. I brought along an old coffee container as my puke bucket to and from treatments. I drifted off to sleep on my way to and from treatments because I was so sleep deprived. My husband drove me to my treatments as he didn't want anyone else to. The poor guy sacrificed his job as he no longer had vacation pay to fall back on, and we had no income coming in. He fed me via my feeding tube the first week I started using it. I can't thank him enough for being my caretaker. Toward the end of my treatments, my youngest sister, Sue; my neighbor Theresa, and my son took turns taking me to treatments.

Chapter 6

DARK DAYS

*D*r. Hare put in an order for a suction machine to help alleviate some of the mucus. I named it my "bedroom buddy." It was small, so I set it up on a tray on the bed next to me. I swear I had that thing going every fifteen minutes throughout the evening. As soon as I got rid of the mucus, it would come back like a gusher a few minutes later. My husband and son took care of emptying the suction machine. And the smell was so offensive. Whenever I tried coughing up the mucus, I ended up making myself puke. Now I was getting less sleep than ever before. I didn't want to live like this. My family would be better off without me. I was worth more dead than alive because of insurance. I worried about the medical bills every night. There were no fundraising benefits for me; nor did I want any. A colleague wanted to put one together for me, but I never got back to her regarding total cost. I was too embarrassed and ashamed to ask for money. It was not fair for my family to go through this, with me hacking, coughing, and puking constantly—and making more medical bills. I was depressed and made people around me miserable. My bedroom became my hiding place, my cave. I could cry there so no one could see me. It seemed I was crying several times a day. I wondered, *Why am I going through this? Is the madness ever going to end?*

The cancer treatments were expensive. Then there were also X-rays, PET scans, MRIs, and so on. I felt I couldn't do this to my family. I couldn't eat because if I tried, I swallowed mucus with my food, and I didn't want to eat thick snot. I finally had it! I got to the point where I didn't care if I lived or not. The Ensure I put through my feeding tube produced more mucus, so I limited my daily intake. After a while, I was not hungry anymore. I was doing well if I got two Ensures in my system a day. Some days it was only one. I was losing weight quickly and was down eighty pounds. I was fortunate that I was overweight and could spare the weight loss. The face mask I had to wear during my radiation therapy was becoming loose from the weight loss. I was informed if I lost more weight, a new mask would have to be made. Treatment would be halted and then have to start over again. I did not want that to happen. Was this ever going to end? I wanted to get back to being normal again.

Dr. Hare tried to entice me during a visit (every Thursday was doctor visit day) with a chocolate chip cookie. I took it home and stared at it. I set it on the kitchen counter and looked at it again. It looked so yummy. I knew that I was not going to eat it. That night, when I got a couple hours of sleep, I dreamed I was chewing on that cookie. Oh, how delicious it was. And I could see my bottom teeth. The dream appeared surreal. I swear I was chewing on that chocolate chip cookie. What I was more than likely chewing on was my fat tongue. My tongue had swelled more due to using my bedroom buddy, which I had quite the nightly affair with. No wonder I was so damn tired. I woke up and realized I was only dreaming. The dream seemed so real. Would I ever be able to eat and taste a warm, gooey, chocolate chip cookie again? The tears started rolling down my cheeks.

The other disgusting thing was that I had to sleep with a hand towel on my pillow because of the mucus that drained out of my mouth when I did get what little sleep I could. It was gross and not pretty. I also had a chubby every morning when I woke up. My tongue would be swollen for about an hour on waking. It was freaky.

During this time, I had ringing in both ears. I thought I was hearing things. This was one of the side effects of treatment, which later stopped for me.

I didn't even try to talk much anymore because of the mucus. I became silent during my trips back and forth between treatments. I was the mucus monster. My iron levels were down, so Dr. Soni had me put liquid iron through my feeding tube. After an hour, I would puke. I also had a lot of heartburn during this time. My grandson wanted to watch me feed myself. I would not allow it, and he would become very upset. A few times I was so tired that I forgot to close the clamp on the tube, so my Ensure came gushing out like a geyser. What a mess. The liquid was all over my clothing. I should have made a video of it and put it on YouTube.

I continued to fix meals for my family and did a little grocery shopping. It was strange to fix meals and not being able to eat them. And hard on me mentally. I smelled the food as I cooked. I can't tell you how hard that was, especially when I knew I couldn't eat any of it. As I shopped, I took pictures with my cell phone of hams, turkeys, steaks, cakes … you name it. At night, as I went to bed, I looked at all the pictures and cried. Oh, how I wanted to eat normal food in the worst way. I dreamed of food often. Food became my obsession! You don't realize what it means to savor and chew food until you can no longer do it. One of the simple pleasures in life!

My final day of radiation and chemo arrived on May 16, 2012. Now I could get back to normal. I was so depressed during my last chemo treatment because the other patients were eating. One older man had a couple salami sandwiches that smelled so darn good. As I pulled the curtain around me to get my feeding tube ready for Ensure, tears streamed down my face. Would I ever be able to eat again? This was so not fair. I heard some people end up living the rest of their lives with a feeding tube. I didn't have breakfast, but this one serving of Ensure would get me through the rest of the day until evening. I felt chilled; I was always so cold. So I wrapped up in my blanket and drifted off for a little nap—until I started hacking, coughing, and spitting up again. I should have bought myself a spittoon and hung it around my neck with a chain.

I have a follow-up appointment with Dr. Soni for Monday and was off for my last radiation therapy. Could I get through this? I had to. As I walked down the hall to the treatment room, I cried. I didn't want to do this, but it was my last one. I sure hoped I didn't need more. I could hardly lie still because of the mucus draining down my throat. The treatment seemed to take forever. But at last I am done and receive my certificate for completing thirty-three treatments. I received hugs from everyone at the center and made a follow-up appointment for the next Thursday to see Dr. Hare. I headed home, thinking now maybe the mucus would stop. Not hardly!

Monday morning arrived, and I saw Dr. Soni for blood work. Soon I could go home and sleep. I couldn't wait. All my blood work was taken from the mediport because my veins had collapsed after chemo. The nurse came back and told me I had to stay the rest of the day and come back the following day because I needed fluids. She told me I was severely dehydrated. I don't recall taking in any water or fluids except Ensure. Oh, come on now; I just wanted to go home. I have had enough of this! As the nurse hooked me up to the IV solution, I began to sob. I was so damn angry. I thought I was done with all this. Talk about depressing. I returned the next day for more fluids, went through the same scenario the following week, and had recurring appointments. My immune system was jeopardized, so I was told to stay away from crowds. I asked about going outside to tend to my rosebushes and other plants; I love gardening. Dr. Soni told me not to because of possible infection.

While at my follow-up appointment with Dr. Hare, I found out my weight loss is still at eighty pounds. He asked if I was getting anything into my throat, to which I responded, "Not at all. I don't like all the mucus." He told me it would take a few weeks to get better. And if I didn't get something down my throat to keep it open, it would eventually grow shut because of the scar tissue that developed during radiation. Dr. Hare was very stern about this and asked if I wanted to live with my feeding tube. I hated the damn thing, even though it was keeping me alive. I thought about how I loved to travel. It sure would be difficult to fly and bring along a case of Ensure or more. Dr. Hare wanted me to try to get something down my throat before I saw him again. I started thinking the remainder of my life would be spent not eating or drinking but receiving all nourishment from my feeding tube.

At home, I tried to swallow. It felt so weird, and I coughed up more mucus. I couldn't do this any longer. My sister and sister-in-law called me, but I didn't want to talk to them because of more mucus. I worked on feeding myself through my feeding tube and then started puking. My husband was watching TV when I started to cry. Sobbing, I screamed, "I have had enough of this shit. I don't want to live! I can't eat or swallow. I talk as if I have a mouthful of marbles. I am a burden to everyone. I hate myself and what I am doing to my family and friends. I am disfigured and feel like a freak show. I feel like damaged goods. I am not worth anything, and God hates me. I don't want to see people for fear I may scare them. My neck is red and oozing. My face appears crooked, as if I had a stroke. I have large scabs on my left forearm and left thigh. I need to lock myself in a closet or hide in the basement. I spit and cough continuously."

My husband became angry and replied, "I thought you were going to beat this. You said in the beginning you were going to fight. Now you are giving up?"

Oh, yes I was because I had enough! I felt I couldn't do this anymore! He had no clue of what I was going through. Nor did anyone else. I yelled at him, "You don't know how hard this is!" My husband was disappointed in me. Well, so was I because I couldn't do this anymore. Enough is enough, damn it! Believe me, I felt sorry for myself many times. Why is the supposed healing taking so long? Dr. Hare suggested antidepressants, but I didn't want any kind of drug. I didn't want to be in la-la land. I truly felt this was never going to end!

I lay awake at night, asking myself if I would be here in a few months, or if I would be joining my mother in the cold, cold ground. I talked to the TV while the *Golden Girls* were on and asked if I would be there to watch them next summer. At times, I was afraid to let myself sleep, thinking I wouldn't wake up the next morning. I would then turn and look at my grandson's picture, with him having the biggest, most beautiful smile ever. Would I be around for him in the future? Would I see him grow up? He was my precious baby. I had to be around for him. I could not give up. I wanted to see him grow up. He needed his grandma. He told me, "When you get better, we can go outside and play." Grandma needed to beat this crap and get better. It was time for my bedroom buddy to suction out the never-ending, copious supply of mucus. Oh, I could hardly wait!

My friend Vicki sent me a Facebook link of a singer who went through oral cancer and had over half his tongue and lymph nodes from his neck removed. As I watched his video, he said his doctor told him he would never sing again. But a couple years later, he was singing beautifully. I cried as I watched and heard him sing. He was such an inspiration. Vicki knew I was beat up, and I believe she sensed I was close to giving up. She knew I needed to see and hear this. This young man went through what I did, and he came through it all. If he could do it, maybe so could I! I had to try. This was the first time I was on my computer. I felt as if I was going to puke. I couldn't believe that I was still so weak.

The next night, before going to bed, I took a sip of water. I was so nervous and almost decided not to try. It was hard to swallow but not so bad. It was such a strange sensation. Something that we do every day without thinking was suddenly difficult, but I did it. The following night, I took a couple more sips and almost gagged. I had to keep trying for my grandbaby. I couldn't give up. I still had a tremendous amount of mucus and a fat tongue. Every night after that, I drank a couple more drops of water and worked myself up to about four ounces.

I always loved to dance. No one was home in early summer, so one afternoon I got out my iPod, turned on some music, and tried dancing. I enjoyed it but felt like I was going to pass out because I was still so weak. I sat down for a minute and then tried dancing again. The second time, though, my damn feeding tube escaped and got loose from the tape. It hung down past the edge of my shirt. It happened several times; I couldn't even get through one complete song. I sat down and cried. Would I ever dance again? My dancing was a stress reliever for me. Then I got on Facebook and posted, "I want to dance again!" My aunt Ella saw my Facebook post and sensed I was down. She called me later to cheer me up.

Chapter 7
DENTAL APPOINTMENTS

$\mathcal{B}$etween treatments, I had several dental checkups at Roswell Park Cancer Institute's Dental Clinic. Because of radiation therapy, my teeth were more prone to cavities. I couldn't open my mouth very wide for cleaning and, of course, couldn't get to my bottom teeth without moving my huge tongue from side to side. I still talked as if I was shot up with novocaine or drunk. My poor dental hygienist, Gwen Tessman, had a heck of a time. She was so patient, gentle, and caring; such a beautiful person inside and out. I am blessed to have her take care of me. I had a prescription toothpaste (Prevident—SF 5000 Plus) to rub on my teeth with disposable oral swabs. I leave it on at night because I cannot brush due to my tongue hiding my bottom teeth. There is still a tremendous amount of swelling.

Every time I went for my checkups, I asked when I could eat normal food again, when the mucus would stop, and when my tongue size would return to normal. I always received the same response: "It will take some time, but soon." Not exactly the words that I wanted to hear. Would it be a couple weeks, a month, or what? I believe I was told this so as not to discourage me and the fact that each person heals differently, depending on the complexity of the surgery, treatments, and side effects.

I saw my dental X-ray while waiting to see Gwen during one

of my appointments. I got out of the chair to get a closer look and noticed twenty or more squiggly things in the left side of my neck. Were those worms or what? I worried because I thought maybe some damn fly laid eggs on my neck during one of my outings, sitting on my front porch. I asked Gwen what they were when she came back into the room. She told me they were staples from my surgery, placed there after removal of my lymph nodes. They will stay in my neck.

Chapter 8
ATTEMPTING TO EAT

I worked myself up to drinking a half-glass of room temperature milk at night, along with a few sips of water. I tried coffee, but it was too acidic and burns. Plus, I couldn't tolerate heat or cold, so everything was room temperature. I tried some chicken broth and got it down as well. Soon, I was drinking my Ensure. However, I continued to accumulate more mucus. Ugh! This continued for a few more months. In June, I was released by the visiting nurses. I was so thankful that I didn't have to get up early any longer. Oh happy day!

I tried walking around my yard a little but still tired quickly. One day I went to Walmart with my family for groceries, toiletries, and so on; I was still not driving at this point. It was going to be a long afternoon for me. I forgot to drink an Ensure before we left and almost passed out in the store. I was so tired. I found a bench and sat down. I viewed the food on the shelves—the fruit, hams, turkeys, veggies, you name it—and wondered, *Will I ever eat these again?*

When we arrived home, I could smell hotdogs roasting on a grill from one of the neighbor's yards. It smelled so damn good! I wanted one. I lay in bed, crying about food I couldn't eat but wanted.

A few family members come for the Fourth of July, and we have a small cookout. I, of course, didn't participate. I stayed inside the house and have some broth and mashed potatoes. I was told to stay away from lots of sunlight due to the radiation on my neck and the scars on my left forearm and thigh. Scars do not like sun. When I went to bed that night (usually 3:00 a.m. or later), I wept secretly as I felt sorry for myself because I couldn't join my family's cookout. I was still having issues with mucus, but not as much. My sister-in-law Donna and her husband, Mike, stayed a few days. Donna made spaghetti for dinner, and I enjoyed sipping the spaghetti sauce, which was my evening meal, along with drinking my Ensure. I was able to taste!

The day arrived when I no longer needed my bedroom buddy. Girls, he wasn't the type of bedroom buddy you would entertain sleeping with you every damn night. Believe me, I tired of him very quickly! I still had a little mucus, coughing, and spitting up. Not pleasant to listen to or watch. A few weeks later, I started to see a few of my bottom teeth. Oh my goodness, I had teeth! I was excited. On my next dental visit, I was told I could start brushing my teeth with my prescription fluoride toothpaste, which I have to leave on and not spit out. Because of all the radiation, my teeth are more susceptible to decay. It seemed, though, that every time I tried to brush, I ended up gagging with dry heaves or puking. Brushing was difficult because even though my tongue was a little smaller, it was still somewhat swollen. I had to do a lot of maneuvering to reach my back teeth. Also, because of the surgery, I could not open my mouth very wide. Even four years later, it takes me more time to brush than normal.

Chapter 9

GRATITUDE FOR DAVID

$\mathcal{I}$ had lots of time to think while I wasn't working. You will understand why I bring up my nephew in my book. I thought back to when my nephew David Hutton passed away September 21, 2005, of injuries sustained in an automobile accident in Pittsburgh in August 2005. David was only twenty-six years old with a very promising career in front of him. He was working toward his doctorate in sports medicine. David was going to school in Pittsburgh and had worked with the Navy Seals and Pittsburgh Pirates. He had such an outgoing and caring personality. David strove to improve the health and well-being of others. I could not understand why God took him. It was very heartbreaking for my brother Tom, and family.

David was a runner and ran in many races. He was such an inspiration and ran with perfect form. Everyone referred to David as "The Machine." His track and field coach, Lynn Newcomer, gave the eulogy at David's funeral. A portion of the eulogy is as follows: "The first thing David will do when he gets to heaven is to go to St. Peter and ask him to measure out a 5K race course." David's objective was to beat his coach's personal 5K best. David was buried with his running shoes and stopwatch. Tom and my nephew, Jeff, made something positive out of a negative. They set up the David Hutton

Memorial Fund 5K Run and 2 Mile Walk that is held every third Saturday in August. This scholarship fund began to benefit Cameron County High School track scholar-athletes but now encompasses surrounding schools. I am so proud of Tom and Jeff. They taught me to make something positive out of something negative; thus, this book. Please check out www.davidhuttonmemorial.org. David's love for running lives on.

Chapter 10

MUM

$\mathcal{I}$ so craved Mum's fudge, which I could not eat. As I sat in bed one evening, I thought about Mum. My mother, Tilly, was a very stubborn German woman. My mother and father, Richard, split up when I was around eleven years old. There were five of us siblings. Mum worked as a bookkeeper in Germany for fifteen years before coming to the United States after marrying my father. She could speak some English but not very well. After they split, she got a job in one of the local factories in Emporium, and from what I heard, she was one of the hardest workers ever. My father moved to California, and Mum raised the five of us on her own.

After her retirement and the death of my nephew David, Mum was diagnosed with breast cancer. It was advanced and terminal. It seemed she broke a bone every year. First, it was one wrist, and the following year, the other wrist. Then she broke her femur. It was a spiral break, and she ended up having a rod put in. David was still living then and helped her with some physical therapy. A few years later, she was in her yard, just watering plants. She turned to the side and thought she heard something snap. Mum's leg hurt some, but she ignored it. Come to find out, she had broken her femur again. It wasn't until later that an X-ray showed it was cracked. By then, it was healing on its own.

Her doctor asked when she had her heart attack. As far as we all knew, she never had one. But a chest X-ray showed she had a heart attack at one point. I truly believe this poor woman suffered a broken heart. Mum never did anything for herself but did the best she could for us. We were her life.

I remember when we were all still very young, she sometimes made us fudge on a rainy day. She would help us to build a makeshift tent using the kitchen table and chairs and a sheet or blanket. Mum never learned to drive. We had wonderful neighbors and friends who drove her to work and back. When they weren't available, she used the local taxi. When it was grocery day, Mum bought each of us a can of soda for Saturday night. Oh, how we looked forward to that treat! Just before school started, we would ride our bicycles into town and meet Mum at the Cabin Kitchen restaurant for a piece of pie. They had the best homemade pies. We then crossed the street and headed to Brown's Boot Shop to try on shoes for school. Those were special days, indeed.

I will never forget when she broke four vertebrae in her back. She tried calling me, but her main telephone (the old rotary type) was on the kitchen wall. The poor woman, lying on her back and pushing herself with her elbows against the floor, made it to her bedroom phone on her nightstand about three hours later and called me. Mum was one tough woman.

It was after that she got the breast cancer diagnosis. She knew something was wrong but never mentioned it. My sister took her for a checkup because she was having difficulty eating and was losing weight. We asked her why she hadn't said something earlier. Her answer was she didn't want to bother anyone, she was old, and figured she would die in her sleep some night. Mum was a proud woman and never wanted to ask for help for anything. What surprised us was that no one in her family ever had cancer. Her family all had heart problems.

Mum finally saw an oncologist. I went with her and my sister Trudie. Her doctor asked us to come into the room to see her left breast. She told him in no uncertain terms that she did not want us looking at her. The poor woman was petrified because we never saw our mother naked. Her breast was almost gone. Her oncologist suggested chemo and radiation. Her cancer was too far advanced for any surgery. The doctor told us treatment would prolong her life for a year, maybe two. She asked all of us if she should go through with it. My answer was that it was not my decision to make. She should do what she wanted to, and I would go along with her wishes. She was hesitant at first but decided to move ahead with treatment. At first, Mum didn't like getting up every day to travel to DuBois for radiation therapy. She took the ATA bus and eventually enjoyed her trips, making friends and seeing other local people going for treatments.

After her treatments were complete and she was home recuperating, she ran into problems. Mum was diabetic, and while taking her insulin out of her refrigerator one morning, she became dizzy and fell. She had awful pain in her back. After the ambulance got her to the hospital, we found out she had broken three more vertebrae in her back. I wished her primary-care physician had checked her for osteoporosis. Mum was in the hospital about a week. Her doctor told us she had three months to live, and she went home via ambulance. She could no longer travel in any vehicle other than ambulance. Her health declined after that episode. Hospice was called in, along with visiting nurses. She had the most wonderful nurses (Amber Beldin and Laura Wall). My siblings and I took turns staying with her between nurse and hospice visits. My sisters stayed during the day, with my brother Tom and his wife, Karen, staying the evenings during the week. I stayed with Mum Friday and Saturday nights and was relieved Saturday and Sunday afternoons. Mum fooled her doctor and us, living almost nine more months instead of the three months we were told.

During my time with her, she told me stories of growing up in Germany during World War II. I heard about the bombings, hangings in her backyard, rationing, and so on. She lived during a rough time and as a young girl, helped out with the Red Cross in her town, Aschaffenburg, where I and my brother Rick were born.

I never appreciated Mum's sense of humor until later in life. She would joke about her cancerous breast, saying she wished a peeping Tom or pervert would look in her window when she was nude and see her mangled, eaten-away breast. She would laugh and say, "He would have a sight to see and would probably never look in anyone's window ever again. That will teach him." I couldn't believe this woman, who was suffering so, could joke about this. But she did and then some. My mum was strong.

Mum had a picture of her siblings on her end table, next to her recliner/rocking chair. She would look at it and say, "It looks like they are waiting for me, doesn't it?" I would reply with a yes. Her brother, my uncle Kurt, was still living, but her sisters were gone (Tante Mai and Tante Barbara). She often brought up that Barbara and she discussed whoever died first would give the other a sign she was okay and what it was like in heaven. She was upset with Barbara because she never received a sign. We talked about giving each other signs.

Mum was tough. I would be in her kitchen, fixing a meal for her, and glance at her. She would wince, and I would ask if she was in pain. Her reply was always no. Damn, I knew the poor woman was in pain, and my heart ached for her. But she never let on she was hurting.

One weekend morning, Mum mentioned looking out of her kitchen window and seeing a young man in her yard. He was dressed in a blue suit and stared at her for a minute. Then he disappeared. She said it was strange because she didn't see him walk away. He just seemed to dissipate into the air. I brought this up in conversation with my siblings. One of them spoke up with, "Oh my God, it must have been David." We hear about loved ones who have passed into the afterlife, coming to greet us before we die. There were other times when Mum mentioned seeing people walking around in her back room. One Friday evening, she kept looking toward her back room (laundry room) and appeared agitated. I got up and closed the door to the laundry room. She settled down.

Toward the end of Mum's life, when I stayed overnight with her on the weekends, I slept on her sofa in the living room. I hooked up my grandson's baby monitor in Mum's bedroom, so I could hear if she needed anything. I used to hear the strangest sounds, as if someone was whispering and then static. But whenever I checked on her, she would be sleeping. She would tell me that a young, beautiful, dark-haired girl would appear just outside her bedroom doorway every night, never crossing the threshold, and smile at her. After I heard that, I became nervous at night and covered up with blankets, peeking around me, fearing I would see someone or something. I never did, though.

The smiling girl never crossed the threshold of Mum's doorway until approximately a week or two before Mum's passing. The hair on the back of my neck seemed to stand up, and I was chilled when Mum told me the young girl finally walked into her bedroom, stood next to her bed, and reached out to her. Mum said it looked like the girl was trying to give her something. Hmmmm? Mum was never delirious and was always aware of her surroundings and what was going on. She wasn't on any powerful prescription painkillers that I was aware of. I knew she took some aspirin at night to help her relax and sleep. Was this girl an angel to accompany my mum on her journey to heaven? We will all find out when it is our time to leave this earth.

On Tuesday, January 22, 2008, I received a phone call from my sister that Karen found mum doubled over in pain in her bathroom. She was put on morphine patches, and one of the hospice nurses told me Mum was going soon. It could be a couple weeks or sooner. That Friday evening, my sister Sue stayed with me and Mum overnight. Sue thought it would be best so I wasn't by myself if Mum passed away. Mum used her walker to get to and from her bedroom to the bathroom and living room to sit in her rocker/recliner. She was in the bathroom and yelled for help, saying she couldn't get up from the toilet. Sue and I went in to help just as she started to fall. We got Mum into bed. She blurted out, "I know I'll never get up and walk again." Mum progressively got worse on Saturday. The hospice nurse said it was a matter of hours. Sue and I called the rest of our siblings and told them time was getting close, and they needed to see her. Mum's friends stopped to see her Saturday evening. She was very alert and coherent. On Saturday, when I was taking a break and my brother Rick was sitting with Mum, he came to fetch me because he couldn't understand what she was saying. Mum was speaking German. Prior to that, she asked to see her firstborn. I don't know why she didn't ask for me by name, because I was her firstborn child. Sunday morning, she was in and out of consciousness. My siblings and I took turns holding her hand, talking to her, and lying in her bed next to her. I was honored to have the privilege to lie next to this woman who worked so hard during her life to give us whatever she could. She was the true "mother." I know she didn't want to leave us. She was afraid my siblings would never keep in contact with each other after she was gone. Mum made me promise that everyone would keep in touch and get together periodically. I continue to have a Fourth of July cookout at my house every year (except in 2012), and a few of my other siblings handle Memorial Day, Labor Day, and Christmas Eve. She loved going to the casino in Salamanca, New York. So around her birthday, March 22, we all try to get together for dinner at the casino in honor of her birthday.

I recall holding Mum's hand and telling her it was okay to leave now. I told her I didn't want her to go. I wished she could stay with me always, but I didn't want her to suffer any longer. I told her that her sisters and Oma and Opa were waiting for her. At times, she looked up at the ceiling and reached toward it. Finally, that Monday afternoon, she passed away. Mum struggled to stay here; I know she was afraid to leave us. She passed as I was holding her hand and telling her it was okay to go … we would all be okay. I still remember so clearly Mum taking her last breath. All my siblings were in the room with us. I have heard the most significant things in life are birth and death. I was blessed to have been with Mum at the time of her death. I tried hard to keep strong because I was the oldest.

I called Amber, the hospice nurse, who contacted the coroner. My siblings all left for home except my youngest sister, Sue. I went into the bathroom to obtain tweezers and a pair of small scissors. Sue thought I had gone bonkers. I proceeded to pluck hairs from Mum's chin, and so on. I had to take care of my mum. She would have had a fit lying in her coffin, thinking people were looking at her chin hairs. Yes, girls, these seem to crop up after menopause. You look for them desperately on a daily basis, and on some days, it appears you don't have any. Then a day later … whoomp, there it is … one stray chin hair about a half-inch long. Now where in the hell did that come from, and why wasn't it there yesterday? I swear these little monsters have some sort of growth hormone in them, such as the beanstalk in *Jack and the Beanstalk*. I hope someone takes care of any facial hair issues I may have when I am gone. Maybe my son will take note of this.

Everyone was gone by the time the coroner and funeral director showed up. My mum looked so small, lying in her bed. Her face didn't look like her any longer. I swear she looked like my opa, her father. It was strange. The coroner couldn't fit the stretcher through the laundry room door because of weird angles, so he came back with a body bag. My heart sank, and I almost screamed no. Even though I knew Mum's spirit was no longer in her body, she always had claustrophobic issues. I watched as her small body was put into the bag and carried to the hearse. I wanted to cry but couldn't. I was glad my siblings were not there to see it.

On the day of the funeral, I got up and said a short tribute to my mum. I choked up a little but stopped myself from crying because I had to be strong. It was a dreary, sunless day. But the strange thing was that several people, including my brother-in-law Brian, mentioned that every time I said Mum's name, the sun would brightly shine, glowing through the stained-glass window behind me. Then it would be gone. Brian told me this only happened when I said, "Mum," or, "Tilly." Was this a message? At the cemetery, Mum's coffin got stuck as it was being lowered into the ground. One of the guys had to jump in part way and get it going again. My brother Rick sort of tapped his foot on the ground and said, "Mom was always a bit stubborn!" We all began to laugh, and I looked around to see who was watching us. I turned around and tried to hide my face, so no one attending would see what an awful daughter I was. Yes, we all knew how stubborn Mum could be. I guess she was letting us know in her own way that she wasn't going into the ground.

Tribute to Tilly

I want to thank everyone for coming today to honor Tilly, our mother, grandmother, great-grandmother, friend, former coworker, and so on. She was not only a mother to us but also had the role of father, raising five of us by herself, stranded in a foreign country, having a very poor knowledge of the English language. Mom always put us before her and went without things to provide for us. She was a strong-willed woman and throughout her disease, never lost her sense of humor, even through her last few days. During her last week with us, she was still giving us orders and still slapping at those ladybugs with her flyswatter on the way to the bathroom at night/early morning.

She was not only my mother but my friend, my hero, and the wind beneath my wings. I thank her for the strong work ethic she instilled in me. Mom surprised us all when she was given only two to three months to live last May and surpassed that. I've never seen such a strong woman, and I am so very proud of her. I will miss calling her every night at nine o'clock and spending the weekends with her. And I will never forget our German heritage, which I and my siblings need to carry on. Rick, my brother, I know you have been doing this.

I want to thank Laura, Amber, Joann, and the hospice/community nurses for helping us through this, friends and family, and a special thank you to Karen for taking care of Mom. Mom asked me a few days ago, while she was still alert, to make certain I thank Karen for her. When Mom was still able to get up at night, Karen was always right behind her. Seeing Mom go downhill the last few days was painful for all of us. I can still see her taking her last breath while I held her hand. She is in a better place and is at peace now with God, her siblings, her parents, and David.

My mother, my friend, my hero, your spirit will always be with us, and we will all miss you. And someday I will see you again. Auf wiedersehen, my beloved mother. I love you!

Chapter 11

DREAMS

$\mathcal{I}$ have heard that young children have psychic abilities but tend to lose them as they grow older. A week or so after Mum's passing, my grandson was with us for the weekend. He was playing in the living room and kept staring into the kitchen and smiling. I could not for the life of me figure out what he was looking at. Kasey was her third great-grandchild and was about twenty-eight months old at the time. He wasn't speaking much. Finally, I asked him what he was looking at. Kasey turned to a family picture of my mum and siblings, pointed to her picture, and smiled. I truly believe she came to visit. Because he was so small and a preemie at birth, Mum called him "the little fella."

A few weeks after Mum's passing, I had two dreams that were so vivid and realistic. The first of which was that my sisters and I were in Mum's house, going through her belongings and cleaning up. As I walked to the laundry room to get to the back door, I noticed a body covered up on Mum's bed. Now, what in the hell was going on? Was one of my sisters playing a prank on me? I approached the bed and realized there was a dead body on the bed. I gasped for air and tried to talk, but I was choking. Finally, I said, "Mum, what, what is going on? You are dead and in the ground. What, What?" I was in shock, wondering how my dead mother could be back in her bed several weeks after she was buried. Suddenly, Mum's hand reached up. She pulled the sheet to uncover her face, opened her eyes, and said clearly, "I'm okay." I immediately woke up. But this couldn't have been a dream. It seemed so damn real.

The second dream I had was that my siblings and I were sitting in Mum's living room. No one sat in her rocker/recliner because that was her chair. We were all sad and discussing things regarding her house. I walked out back for a breather and stood looking out the laundry room window. Suddenly, I saw movement. Someone was behind one of the small pine trees on the hill behind the house. As this person came forward, I realized it was Mum. Hmmm? She's dead, so what in the hell was going on? As she came down the hill, she walked perfectly, with no limp. She was smiling and looked so young. I ran to the living and shouted to my siblings that Mum was walking down the hill toward the house. We were in shock, to say the least! When Mum was alive, she always came into the house through the back door into her laundry room. Seldom did she come in the front door. On this particular night, she entered the house through the front door, walked past us, and sat in her rocker/recliner. We all looked at her and tried to speak. I stuttered with, "Mum, what are … you … doing here? You are … dead." She replied with, "I never left." I woke up, sweating and breathless. What was going on? It was a dream, yet it didn't appear to be a dream. It was so realistic, I swear I heard her voice!

The last message I received from Mum came shortly before Easter in 2008. My sister Sue ("Susie Snowflake" as I call her at times) called me while she was at Mum's house, cleaning up. She asked if I remembered ever planting flowers behind the small shed. My response was no because who would see them? We planted flowers for Mum in front of her house. Mum's favorite rose color was yellow. At that time of the year, roses were not in bloom. What Sue told me next was astonishing. There was one yellow tulip behind the shed. Perhaps a bulb through the years somehow transported back there from the front of the yard. I didn't recall planting yellow tulips in front of the house. I truly believe it was a message from our mum.

I attend the butterfly release put on by community nurses at the hospital every August in St. Marys, Pennsylvania. I let a monarch butterfly loose in the air in honor of my mum. It is a special event. An individual plays the bagpipes, which always brings tears to my eyes. The first year after I lost my mum, I talked to one of the nurses about my dreams of Mum and the yellow tulip. This sweet nurse had visited my mother on a few occasions. I asked if I was going nuts because of the vivid, realistic dreams. Her reply was no. She was also a hospice nurse and told me that our loved ones who have passed on send messages to the living. She then mentioned there were many stories of this happening, and I was not nuts.

The next day, I thought more about this and remembered Mum and I discussing the apparent fact Aunt Barbara never messaged her after her death to let Mum know she was okay. Mum and I did talk about her letting me know. I used to worry about Mum and miss her so much. Now I realize she was sending me messages through my dreams and the one yellow tulip that she was fine. The dreams were not frightening but comforting to me. My mum was safe and no longer suffering.

Mum had told me she so loved to dance. Her aunt in Aschaffenburg owned a restaurant and bar. Mum helped periodically and entered dance contests, usually winning. The town had a yearly carnival, and she entered its dance contests, too. Mum told me about some of the prizes she won, such as bottles of liquor and wine. Throughout all the many years I knew her, I never got to see this special woman dance. One thing I do know for certain is that when it is time for me to leave this earth, I will be dancing with my mum! When I dance, I feel as if I am in another world, dimension/plane, with no cares in the world. And I do dance like no one is watching. If you want a high, dance, don't do drugs!

Chapter 12

IS THERE A LIGHT AT THE END OF THE TUNNEL?

*T*oward the middle of August, I decided to try to return to work after Labor Day. Like a beginner, I practiced driving to town and back. On the first few trips, I was nervous and experienced dry heaves. Then I drove to meet my boss at the time, which was a little more than an hour away. I felt shaky halfway there and had to stop at one point and vomit due to coughing. But I made it there and back safely.

On my first day back to work, I was so nervous I had dry heaves. It was a good thing my office was away from the other offices and clerical desks. I was constantly hacking and coughing, and I went through Kleenex so fast that I should have bought stock in the company. Yes, I still dealt with mucus. It wasn't as bad but still lingered. I brought my Ensure to have for lunch, and sometimes I bought soup. I also ate a lot of ice cream then and some soft foods. I was finally maintaining my weight.

On my travels back and forth to work, I listened to my Sirius/XM radio and iPod. I tried singing to certain songs, such as "The Warrior"; "Try, Try, Try"; and "Stronger (What Doesn't Kill You)." Believe me, my singing was not pretty, but it certainly helped with my speech and made me feel stronger in spirit.

I also read to my grandson to practice speaking. It's a good thing he was young, and didn't understand what I was saying. An adult, if listening, would wonder, *What is she saying?*

My next appointment with Dr. Arshad was in the beginning of October. As I sat in the waiting room, the receptionist asked an older patient for his green card. I commented that we were all members of the Green Card Club at Roswell. Every new patient is issued a plastic green card with his or her name and patient number. I am a proud holder of this particular card.

I had a good checkup with Dr. Arshad. We discussed my feeding tube because I was told earlier in the year that if I maintained my weight, I could have it removed. I reminded Dr. Arshad of this, and that if it wasn't removed, I was going trick-or-treating with it not taped up but hanging out, and I would walk up and down the street, twirling it in my hands. I would go as a Martian. I then pointed my finger at my doctor and told him not to be making plans for me because I was going on vacation in the spring. It was a wonder I didn't get thrown out of his office. I was to contact Dr. Hare, who would make arrangements with Dr. Mancl to have my feeding tube removed.

The day arrived to see Dr. Mancl. My sister Sue went with me. I assumed that I would be put to sleep or receive a local anesthetic in my stomach area. I was wrong. Dr. Mancl explained that it would only take a minute or less and to hold onto her assistant's hand. I was told it would hurt, but only for a few minutes. She counted to three and yanked out the feeding tube. Blood squirted out. I didn't make a sound. It smarted like a rubber band snapping but ten times more. Sue said I should have seen the look on my face. Dr. Mancl was right; it quit hurting after a few minutes. The small hole required no stitches, only a bandage. I was told not to eat or drink for a few hours because it would come back through the hole, which had to heal from the inside out. My sister asked if I could drive. Well, hell yes! It was great to have that damn thing out of me. I drove back to my office and worked the rest of the day. A few people I worked with said they would have gone home to recuperate. Believe me, this was nothing compared to what I went through with surgery and radiation side effects. The next thing to work on was getting the mediport removed.

That first Thanksgiving, in 2012, I ate some mashed potatoes loaded with gravy. My family and I were visiting my sister-in-law Donna for the holiday. My father called me in the evening to wish me a happy Thanksgiving and told me to eat some turkey. He said, "I know you can do it." I couldn't that year, but it got easier every year. When I went to visit him in the fall of 2013, he made me toast and told me, "You can eat this." I tried a little, but it was rough on my tongue. I thank him for pushing me. It was then that I decided to write a book.

Over the next few months, the doctors continued to assure me everything was fine. Finally, I went on a cruise in March 10, 2013, with friends to Panama City, Panama; Aruba; and Cartagena, Columbia, to name a few of the places. I was so thankful that I could go on this cruise. I was a little apprehensive because the only places I went after my cancer episode were to work, the grocery store, and to visit family. I was going out of the country. I was sad that my friend Bea couldn't join us that year. We arrived a day before our cruise and booked a room at a local hotel. We couldn't get into our room immediately. Jeri was at the front desk, checking us in. Cherie and I had to use the bathroom, but we had no room yet. Cherie contacted one of the hotel maids to tell her we needed a restroom, but Jeri was still at the front desk. We gave the maid the room number that was being assigned to us. The maid was kind enough to let us in the room. We both used the bathroom and then Cherie went downstairs to meet Jeri. I sat out on the balcony with my feet propped up, enjoying the scenery. The girls returned and knocked at the door urgently, so I let them in. Come to find out, I was in the wrong room! I got out of there quickly.

The ports were beautiful. Cartagena was a little scary, though, because military police were all over the streets. We were told not to venture alone into the jungle area. Aruba had the coolest-looking old trees. They were called divi-divi trees. I got to see the Panama Canal, which is very impressive. Bonaire was the most beautiful in my eyes. The salt flats were amazing, with white and pink sands of salt. I loved watching the flamingos, as well. The island of Curacao was breathtaking, with its colorful houses of yellow, teal, pinks, and blues. It was so picturesque. We did a lot of walking and sightseeing. It is interesting to learn about the history and cultures of other countries. I felt alive again.

I ate mostly the desserts and soups, and I frequented the ice cream machine in the pool area several times daily. I certainly didn't get my money's worth of food that year but was grateful I could eat what I could. Our waiters in the main dining room during dinner were a little surprised that I didn't eat much. Cruises are for eating, and Royal Caribbean has the best food. The waiters were so kind and asked if they could bring me more to eat. They did their best to oblige me. I was full, though, from soups and desserts. But I was so hungry in the evenings. I couldn't go to sleep with gnawing hunger pangs, so ordered two cups of hot cocoa from room service every night before retiring.

I ran into a problem with customs on the way home at the DC airport. The agent looked at my passport and said, "That's not you." I was eighty pounds heavier before my cancer. I told him I lost a lot of weight, and that was what cancer did to me. He apologized and let me through.

Things were going good until I was laid off from my position of close to twenty-four years in April of 2013. I was devastated because I had worked many hours of overtime, giving my job well over 100 percent. I was a salaried employee. My employer mentioned in March that there might be layoffs, but I felt it really didn't apply to me. I was there longer than anyone. When I heard the news, I almost fainted and was nauseated. I thought, *This can't be true after everything I have went through! What more bad things can happen to me?* I was ashamed and embarrassed to have to tell my family that I was such a loser. I was so devastated. My family relied on me to help pay the bills. I was so upset because I could lose my house and vehicle. I also had exorbitant medical bills to pay. My grandson also lived with me during the school year. I came home and told my husband. He asked if I could receive unemployment benefits, which I can. However, the money is not enough to cover my house, vehicle, and utility payments. What was I going to do?

I headed to bed and cried before finally drifting off to sleep for maybe an hour. I woke up and began crying again. I couldn't seem to stop. For a week, I only crawled out of bed to use the bathroom. Nor did I eat. I was constantly crying. I didn't shower or change my clothes. I was at a loss. I felt humiliated, like I was slapped in the face. I was a failure. I wanted and needed to work. I heard that stress and depression can cause cancer. The more I thought about it, I decided I had fought too damn hard to get to where I was after treatments, and I was not going to let this upset me any longer. I was worth something. I told myself that I would find work. A good friend, Myrna, told me of a job opening. After three weeks, I had a new job. It seems that when one door closes, God opens another door.

My next appointment was in June of 2013 for a PET scan and follow-up with Dr. Arshad. The PET revealed something around my sinus area. I brought up my seasonal allergies with sneezing, and so on. He had me go down the hall to another doctor for another test. Oh no, not the roto rooter test again! Dang, I should have checked myself that morning for any nostril hair sticking out. Once again, my right nostril got sprayed with a slight numbing agent and tube inserted with a small camera down my nose and into my throat. Whatever eye makeup I have on was gone from the tears streaming down my face. I was gagging, and so on. It was the weirdest sensation ever. I was so nervous that I was almost shaking. Dr. Arshad came into the room and checked the computer screen, reviewing the scan.

Finally, he reported no cancer, but he saw a lot of mucus and swelling of sinus cavities. Exactly what I predicted. I cannot begin to describe the feeling of exhilaration when I heard the words, "no cancer." I could live again! I brought up to Dr. Arshad that Dr. Soni told me if I was cancer-free in a year, I could have the mediport removed. He said he would let Dr. Soni know I could have it removed. I told him I was sick and tired of looking like I had a third nipple sticking out whenever I wore a stretchy or slinky top or dress. Poor Dr. Arshad shook his head. He was probably thinking, *Please get her the hell out of here!*

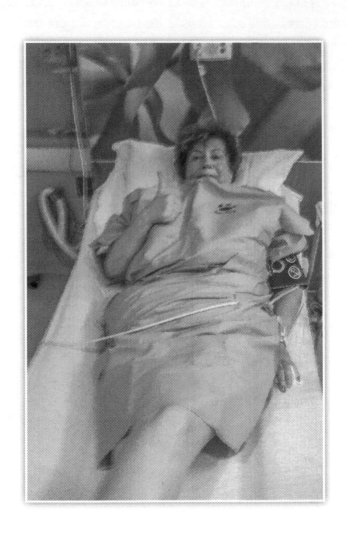

Chapter 13
BYE, BYE, MEDIPORT

*F*inally, at the end of August, I headed back into surgery at Olean General Hospital for removal of my mediport. Prior to the surgery, I bought a Kritter Keeper (a small, plastic, see-through container that looks like a small aquarium but to put bugs in). Dr. Mancl would be doing the surgery, and before going in, I asked if I could please have the mediport so I could take a picture of it. She would try to do it, but if not, when I came in for my post-op checkup, she would have one so I can take a quick picture. If she could get mine, I could keep the little devil. I had never been so excited for a surgery in my life.

While waiting in pre-op, I urged the attending nurse to "Let's get the show on the road." I tried to get a selfie with a thumbs-up while the nurse was trying to get an IV in. I was so bad. At last, I was wheeled into the operating room. I couldn't get there soon enough. Waiting were several nurses and an anesthesiologist. Dr. Mancl mentioned that I wouldn't be put to sleep completely but would be in a dreamlike state. Country music was playing. I asked if they could change the channel because I was not a big fan of country. I do like some of the older songs, but country is not my preference. I prefer lively dance music/top hits. One of the nurses changed the station, and "Radioactive" is playing by Imagine Dragons. I shout out with,

"That was me a while ago. I was radioactive!" I swear I had everyone in the room laughing. Then I got tired but kept talking.

A week later, I met with Dr. Mancl for my post-op appointment. I walked into the office with a Walmart shopping bag. You should have seen the looks I got from the receptionist and nurses. When I saw Dr. Mancl, she handed me my mediport in a plastic bag. I was so thrilled! I told her I brought my Kritter Keeper to get a picture of the mediport in it, in case she wouldn't let me keep it. She told me I was good to go and that we had a nice conversation during surgery. I asked what we talked about, but she replied with only, "We had a nice conversation."

Chapter 14

THE SIMPLE THINGS

I had a follow-up appointment with Dr. Arshad close to April Fool's Day in 2014. I told him I was going to get my tongue pierced. Oh, my goodness. I could see the shock on his face and imagine seeing the gears in his brain churning at an alarming rate. He was probably thinking, *I spent fourteen hours in surgery to rebuild your tongue, and you are wrecking it.* I looked at him and blurted out, "April Fools!"

I finally broke down and had my first mammogram when I was fifty-eight. I was, to say the least, a nervous wreck. The technician was a very young woman. I didn't know what to expect when she placed tape with what appeared to be a little silver ball on each nipple. I asked her, "Now what do I do, get up and dance?" The poor woman looked shocked and replied, "No, ma'am." She sure got me out of there in a hurry. I didn't mean to scare her. I was just amusing myself because I was nervous.

Yes, we take the simple things in life for granted, myself included, before cancer. The simple things, which are the big things in my life, are as follows.

breathing
swallowing
talking

eating

smell

touch

the wonderment of a child's eyes on Christmas morning and his or
her innocence

a child's laughter

a newborn's cry

the sound of rain hitting a rooftop

the smell of freshly mowed grass

the twinkling stars in the night sky

the kaleidoscope of colors of the leaves on trees in the fall

the smell of dirt while planting a garden

the first snowflake of winter

the birds singing on a spring morning

the echo of a train whistle on a cool, crisp night

listening to the spring peepers in the evening

the smell of the earth after rain on a summer day

a rainbow

crickets chirping on a summer/fall night

the first bloom of a rose, or any flower

geese honking as they head south for the winter or return in the spring

the sound of silence

food and water

waking up every day

Epilogue

I could go on and on. Enjoy these simple things because they are, in reality, the big things in life. And until we go through something as drastic as cancer and face our mortality, we often don't realize how precious they are. So take time out to fully envelop these before it is too late. Enjoy your family, and live life to the fullest—as if each day was your last. Don't procrastinate on taking a trip or whatever your wishes may be. Just do it! You don't want to look back and think, *Damn, I should have.* Life is too short.

I was told that more than likely, I would never eat bread again because most people who have gone through what I did never regain their ability to create saliva. I don't have the saliva I used to, but I do have what I need. If I had difficulty eating a certain food, I tried again in a month, and it became easier every month. I am eating bread, rolls, sandwiches, subs, and so on with lots of water. Remember, you can't keep bread away from this German girl! I can also eat nuts. I still have difficulty with pork, chicken breast, turkey breast, and other dense meats. Mozzarella cheese is also difficult. Another thing my doctors told me was that I probably wouldn't eat hamburger or any ground meat again. The texture does not appeal to most patients. I have had hamburger, but I was never a big fan of hamburger.

Because the floor of my mouth was raised during my surgery, particles of food usually become trapped under the left side of my tongue and is a bugger to clean out. But don't tell me what I can't eat because I will prove you wrong. I eat much slower now but savor every damn bite I shove in my mouth and drink lots of water with my food. My throat is smaller due to radiation scars, so I can only eat small bites of food at a time. Dr. Soni mentioned I could have my throat stretched to make it easier to swallow bigger portions of food. Good Lord no! I would be three times the size I am today and eating with reckless abandonment. If you are having a meal with me, please be patient with the amount of time it takes me to eat. I spend a great deal of time chewing and am messy. But most important, I can eat!

In retrospect of what all transpired, I consider myself extremely lucky. Ever since my ordeal, I notice the grass is greener, the leaves on the trees in fall are so much brighter, the snow is more glistening, the sun is more brilliant, and the sky much bluer. Even dark clouds in the sky have a beautiful shade of gray. I even welcome the rain and enjoy listening to it as it hits the roof and nourishes the earth. A while back, when I heard the birds chirping on a spring morning or the early spring peepers, I wondered if it was my last year to hear these wonderful sounds. No, I have survived to enjoy these and to see my precious grandson's smile. Cancer isn't funny, but if I didn't laugh throughout this time, I would no doubt be crying. And though I cried a lot in the past, I now laugh more. Laughter is good medicine for the soul. Whenever I was nervous or scared, I cracked jokes. That was how I tolerated what I was experiencing.

My heartfelt thanks go out to Dr. Hassan Arshad and staff, Dr. Gupta, Elizabeth McNamara, Roberta, the nurses on the seventh floor at Roswell Park during February/March of 2012, Gwen Tessmann, Dr. Hare, Dr. Soni, and Dr. Mancl. Without your expertise and care, I would not be in the position I am today. I also want to thank my husband (my caretaker), my son (my second caretaker and for always making me laugh), Vicki (for believing in me, traveling with me to doctors' appointments, and assisting me with my book), Bea (for sending me inspirational messages and e-mails), family, and friends. I apologize if I left anyone out. You are all awesome!

Several people I have known with oral, head, and neck cancer have passed away. Do I feel guilty because I am still living? Of course I do. It eats at me at times. I feel like one of those people who was a survivor in a plane crash. Almost everyone is gone except me. My good friend Vicki tells me the reason is because God is not done with me yet, and I need to get my book out. Yes, cancer is bad, but it was also a blessing in disguise for me. I learned to be somewhat patient, to slow down, and to stop and smell the roses. I lost weight that I needed to and reconnected with past friends and my father. I felt sorry for myself many times and asked, "Why me?" I learned not to look at a glass as half empty, but half full … no, full! Now I know why this happened to me. I believe things do happen for a reason, and mine was to send a message to others. I know this sounds crazy. However, I have learned I can help others who are going through this. There is a higher power out there … God. My sense of humor, faith, stubbornness, and determination helped me through my battle.

I know most cancer survivors wonder, *Will my cancer come back?* Every time you feel a little pain, you wonder, *Is my cancer back?* I know cancer survivors sometimes have post-traumatic stress disorder. This happens more often when it is time for scans. We absolutely cannot continue to live our life thinking these what-if thoughts every single day. I know some are nervous; as am I. But I have learned to relax and be positive that all is good. You have to go on and live each day to the fullest. This applies not only to cancer survivors but to all of you.

I compare myself now to an old wine glass—discolored and a little chipped around the edges with my scars. A former coworker who looked at the gap on the underside of my left forearm about seven months after my surgery mentioned it was weird looking, and he could see the outline of the bone. He suggested that perhaps I should keep it covered. I was extremely embarrassed at first and did cover it for a few months with elastic bandages. My nephew Jeff Hutton is a certified athletic trainer/physical therapist who gave me exercises to strengthen my arm. I can now do everything I did with my arm

71

prior to surgery. Thanks so much, Jeff! Hell no, I am not keeping it covered! It is one of my many battle scars that, without a doubt, I am proud of. And it is truly a conversation piece.

I also wore scarves around my neck to conceal how the left side looks so different than the right side. Now I let it all hang loose. I don't care what anyone thinks. It adds to my personality.

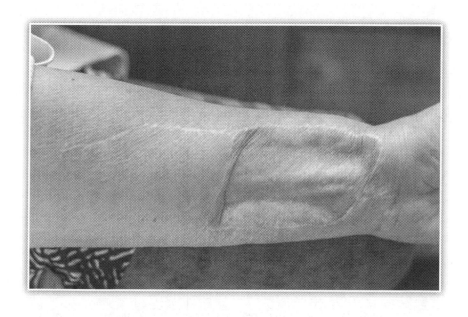

I also have scars on my neck with discoloration from radiation, a scar from trach tube, scar on my stomach from the feeding tube, scar from mediport on my chest, and a scar from skin graft on my left thigh. I also have scar tissue that you can't see in my throat from radiation, which prevents me from eating big bites of food. At times I choke on a vitamin E gel cap, especially if it goes down sideways. But I have learned to live with it. I have several titanium staples hidden in my neck as well as a scalloped tongue. Yes, I have a fancy tongue. I am so fancy! You have heard the song "I'm So Fancy"? Yes, that's me and my tongue! As I mentioned earlier in my book, I was never a thing of beauty, and now my scars give me personality. I am the same person but stronger with a greater value and appreciation of life, and the urge to help others going through oral, head, and neck cancer.

I reconnected with my father and am happy I did. Do not hold grudges as life is too short. I got through this, and so can you. Don't live with a "poor me" attitude. We all have some rain that has fallen on our lives, and we have all made mistakes. We are human. I have lost family members and grew up in a broken family, along with other issues. So many people blame their drug habits, alcohol problems, and criminal records on being brought up in a broken home or being abused mentally and physically as a child. I went through all of that. Yes, I thought I was to blame, but not anymore. Going through everything has been a learning experience and made me a stronger person. Be thankful with what you have. Keep a positive outlook on life. Life is what you personally make of it!

Since my cancer episode, my life hasn't been about waiting for the thunderstorms to stop. Rather, it's about dancing in them. I went through one hell of a storm and came out dancing. I almost named my book *To Hell and Back*. Do not take the simple things in life for granted.

When things get tough in life, and you encounter a bump in the road, think positive thoughts, and ...

Just Dance!

The Dancing Queen

I want to convey to anyone going through oral cancer that you may not experience the side effects I had or endure the surgery and treatments I did. It all depends on the stage and severity of the disease. Every person heals differently. It took me a long time to be able to eat, but it may not for you. You can get through this; there is a light at the end of the tunnel. Never ever give up hope. Believe in yourself and God. Stay positive and laugh lots. Stand up, raise your arms to shoulder level, spread your legs slightly, look toward the sky, and yell, "Cancer, get out of my body. You have no business being inside me, and you are not the boss of me. I am in control. This is my body. Leave now, and don't ever come back!" Yes, I did that on several occasions.

I know you will feel like crying at times. Let the tears flow. Watch comedies and spend time with friends. Some people may hesitate to be around you for fear of not knowing what to say. Enjoy time with your family. My healing took time; much longer than I ever expected. Ultimately, I had to learn patience. It will eventually get better. My tongue will never be like it was prior to surgery. And at times, it feels foreign. I have a new norm. But damn, it works! It took time to learn to maneuver food around to eat. I count my blessings every day because I can talk, and I can eat. Such are the simple things in life!

If you are in need of someone to talk to or any emotional support, please contact me. I didn't have anyone to discuss what I was going through with because no one in my area went through oral cancer. I stopped talking to my family while traveling to and from treatments. For one, because they had no idea of what I was feeling or going through. And second, all the damn mucus. I wish there had been someone like me who could have helped me through this. Again, I do believe things happen for a reason, and perhaps I was chosen to go through what I did to gain knowledge of this dreaded disease, to lend support to others going through this similar cancer, and to appreciate the simple things in life. I will laugh with you and cry with you. You can contact me at justdanceagainstoralcancer@gmail.com.

About the Author

Christine Dickinson worked in several positions, including twenty-four years for an attorney/abstract company. Dickinson was the first female president of the Northern Appalachian Landman's Association. She is now self-employed. Dickinson and her husband, John, have one son and one grandson and live in Emporium, Pennsylvania.

Printed in the United States
By Bookmasters